PIAZZA

"I knew New York was where

I was meant to be."

—Mike Piazza

DAILY  NEWS

Published by Sports Publishing, L.L.C.
www.SportsPublishingLLC.com
www.dailynewsbooks.com

PIAZZA

DAILY ⊡ NEWS

VICTORIA J. MARINI, Coordinating Editor

JOSEPH J. BANNON JR., Supervising Editor
JULIE L. DENZER, Interior and Dustjacket Design
ERIC MESKAUSKAS AND ANGELA TROISI, Photo Editors
JULIE L. DENZER AND CHRIS CARY, Photo Production
JEFF IGNATIUS AND DAVID HAMBURG, Copyediting/Proofing

THE NEW YORK DAILY NEWS, Front & Back Cover Photos

ISBN 1-58261-358-3

Sports Publishing, L.L.C.
www.SportsPublishingLLC.com
www.dailynewsbooks.com

Printed in the United States.

PHOTO CREDITS

ACKNOWLEDGMENTS

When Mike Piazza took his place behind home plate for the first time as a New York Met, *Daily News* readers had a front-row seat for his much-anticipated debut. Through the paper's award-winning writing and unmatched photography, *Daily News* readers were able to join in the cheers when Piazza starred—and groan with the boos when he slumped. And as the Mets' roller-coaster 1999 season wound its way to the Piazza-led playoff drama that had all of New York talking about a possible subway series, the *Daily News* was there with its unique insight into New York's newest baseball superstar.

Bringing this story to life each day in the pages of the *Daily News* took the hard work and dedication of many people at the paper. When we first approached the *Daily News* about this project, we received the overwhelming support of Les Goodstein (Executive Vice President/ Associate Publisher) and Ed Fay (Vice President/Director of Editorial Administration). Among the others at the paper who were instrumental in assisting us in this project were John Polizano, Lenore Schlossberg, Eric Meskauskas, Mike Lipack, Angela Troisi, Vincent Panzarino and Faigi Rosenthal and her great staff. From the *Daily News* sports department, we specifically want to acknowledge the support of editor Leon Carter.

Space limitations preclude us from thanking all the writers and photographers whose contributions appear in this book. However, wherever available, we have preserved the writers' bylines and the photographers' credits to ensure proper attribution for their work.

Finally, I am grateful for all the support and effort of those at Sports Publishing Inc. who worked tirelessly on this project: Julie L. Denzer, Joe Bannon Jr., Terry N. Hayden, Susan McKinney, Chris Cary, Claudia Mitroi and David Hamburg.

—*Victoria J. Marini*
    Coordinating Editor

After the Mets won Friday night,

I called the Elias Sports Bureau and got these numbers:

The Mets were averaging 18,177 fans

before [Mike Piazza joined the team].

Since then,

they are averaging more than 35,000.

You do the math.

—*Mike Lupica*

September 6, 1998

Piazza
TABLE OF CONTENTS

Piazza

TABLE OF CONTENTS

ONE MAN'S IMPACT

May 24, 1998

"One guy. One guy did this."

—*NY police officer Jimmy Murphy on
the crowds at Piazza's Met debut*

Less than an hour before the game, the lines to buy tickets near Gate E were still trying to back up to Roosevelt Ave. as the people kept coming down the steps from the elevated platform, the way they used to.

The crowd would eventually be 32,900 at Shea Stadium, but on this day it would look like more, and sound like more. Hope always seems to pad the house. Mike Piazza was behind the plate and batting third and on the Saturday before Memorial Day, New York was alive with the National League again.

"One guy," Jimmy Murphy, one of the cops at the Diamond Club entrance, said at 3:30, watching the walk-up crowd keep coming off the trains and out of the parking lot.

"One guy did this."

Who knows what the crowd would have been like without Piazza? Who knows

what the rest of the season would have been like?

"This one here is a little bit out of the old days," Jimmy Murphy said.

We were on our way to the loge, Box 362, over third base. There were three

boys of my own, and a friend of the oldest boy. They did not want to watch the

Pacers-Bulls yesterday, or watch the Yankees-Red Sox on television. They wanted to

see Piazza's first game as a Met. This had all been decided yesterday morning.

A wonderful walk-up baseball Saturday in New York.

Finally it was time for the game. Finally Piazza was walking to the plate in the bottom of the first, and it was here that all the pre-game cheers he had heard were turned into whispers. The cheer he got now started high in the upper deck, in the sun, picked up steam through the shadows, where we were, then exploded again around Piazza standing in all the sun at home plate.

He grounded out and then struck out, but in the fifth he pounded an RBI double up the alley in right-center and took third on the throw to the plate, and this was a bigger explosion than before, because this was the season he was supposed to bring with him from Florida. **This was what everyone had come out to the ballpark to see, and feel.**

One guy.

One guy in sports can still change a season.

Maybe even this one.

Maybe it doesn't always have to be the Yankees in New York, the way it has been lately. It wasn't all Yankees even when they were breaking all the records, winning everything there was to win. They didn't own New York when the Dodgers and Giants were still here, and they sure didn't own it in the 1980s, when the Mets were winning a World Series and drawing home crowds of three million a season, something the Yankees have never done.

As wonderful as this Yankee team is, full of possibilities and the chance to make history, what we know in New York is that nothing lasts forever, on either side of town. Now Piazza is on the Mets' side and there is a rumor that the Mets might make a play for Robin Ventura of the White Sox, maybe even Albert Belle.

If the Mets get going good now, if Piazza hits the way he can and picks everybody up, imagine what Shea will sound like when the Yankees come in there in a month. Imagine the echoes, out of the '80s, out of '69, out of National League New York. We heard those echoes in Box 362 yesterday, up in the loge, third-base side. **Everybody heard at Shea.**

MIKE, METS ARE STORMIN'

May 30, 1998

"I've never seen anything like it, so I can't explain it. It's different, and it's a good difference."

—Bobby Valentine

BY THOMAS HILL

Exactly two weeks after he left the Dodgers, and one week after he joined the Mets, Mike Piazza finally came home last night. He showed his family something special, too: a sleek new team that has become his vehicle to success.

The Piazza Express continued its extraordinary run as the Mets pounded the Phillies, 11-0, at the Vet. The Mets extended their winning streak to seven games, their longest since August 1992, and achieved their fifth straight victory since Piazza came aboard.

"I've never seen anything like it, so I can't explain it," Mets manager Bobby Valentine said. "It's different, and it's a good difference."

Two of the Mets' six shutouts have come with Piazza behind the plate, a startling development for a catcher whose reputation with the Dodgers was as something less than a pitch-calling savant. Rick Reed, who shook off Piazza just

twice all night, seemed pleased with their first combined effort. Valentine praised Piazza's "retention" of thoughts about hitters, as well as his rapid adjustment to a new staff.

"I always thought the toughest thing to happen in baseball was to have a new catcher come to a team," Valentine said. "I thought that was the most disruptive thing that could happen to a team. That's just my opinion. **I guess it's just the quality of this guy."**

Piazza, who grew up in suburban Philadelphia and rooted for the Phillies as a child, was 1-for-4 with an RBI single and two runs scored—including the Mets' fourth run in the fifth, when he eluded a tag at the plate.

The Mets matched their season high with 16 hits—their fifth straight game with 11 or more hits since Piazza arrived. They have averaged 7.8 runs in Piazza's first five games, and allowed an average of just 2.2.

"I wasn't so sure about the ripple effect," Valentine said. "But I don't believe in coincidences."

Newman? No, PIAZZA!

Chapter 3

IT'S BOOS FOR MIKE

July 21, 1998

"You go through times when you get in a little bit of a rut. Every hitter has gone through it. Last year was a career year for me, where everything went right, and it's tough to measure up to that."

—Mike Piazza

BY BILL MADDEN

It is still maybe a trifle too soon to declare that the Mike Piazza era at Shea is over. But the honeymoon sure is.

OK, it was the Pirates on a Monday night, at the same time the Yankees were home for the first time in two weeks. Still, there were only 18,088 out at Shea to root on a Mets team that supposedly is very much in the thick of the wild-card race. The same Mets team that supposedly underwent a major transfusion of credibility and rejuvenation when it acquired Piazza from the Marlins for three top minor-league prospects May 22.

Those extra 10,000-15,000 fannies in the seats Piazza initially accounted for are fast disappearing.

Kind of like the Mets' bogus wild-card dreams. And those who did "show up at Shea" last night made their presence felt mostly by booing Piazza.

They booed him when he lined out to second with the bases loaded and no-body out in the first. They booed him louder when he struck out to end the fifth with Brian McRae left stranded at first base. And when the Pirates executed

successive steals of second base in the eighth—the latter on a pitchout—they really

booed him. His strikeout to begin the bottom of that inning was merely their cue to

start heading for the parking lot.

We have sure come a long way since May 22, when Shea seemed so full of life

for the first time in such a long time, thanks to Piazza, and so, too, did the Mets.

Since then, the Mets are 24-26 and have dropped a notch in the standings to third.

Piazza is hitting .329 as a Met, but even he acknowledges that it is a hollow .329

and probably deserving of the fan backlash nobody could possibly have envisioned a

month ago.

"It's not   the most productive .330," Piazza said, forcing a

smile. "I'll be   the first to say that. I'm not exactly rip-

ping the   cover off the ball. I'm not hitting

the ball the way I know I have.

I'm my own worst critic."

When it was suggested to him that maybe the

Shea fans might be just a tad worse, he shook his head.

"I understand the situation," he said. "It's really frustrating for me right now,

and it's compounded by the fact that

we're not playing well."

His partner in crime, Todd Hundley,

concurred. Together, they struck out

five times in seven at-bats last night,

leaving a total of six runners on

base—and Hundley heard his share of boos, too.

"It just goes to show you that the two of us can't carry

this team," Hundley said.

Apparently not. But that was sure the hope. The offense, which sputtered along and spit out just enough runs in April and May to complement superior starting pitching and defense, was finally provided the middle-of-the-order presence it so desperately lacked when Piazza came over from his Florida pit stop. Hundley's return from the disabled list was the other half of the ticket to the playoffs.

"You go through times when you get in a little bit of a rut," Piazza said. "Every hitter has gone through it. **Last year was a career year for me**, where everything went right, and it's tough to measure up to that."

He's right about that. But in turning down $85 million from the Dodgers,

forcing them to trade him, he essentially put himself in the position of having to

measure up to that, to prove he is worth the $100 million his agent is seeking for

him.

He hasn't proved it to the Met fans who once em-

braced him and now are booing him. More important, he hasn't

proved it to the Mets brass, which must soon decide whether to become the dumper

or the dumpee in the "shoot the moon" trading deadline sweepstakes. In the club-

house last night, GM Steve Phillips and his

assistant, Omar Minaya, wore somber faces and

tight lips.

Up until these past couple of days, their

hearts were telling them that Piazza—and

maybe Hundley as well—would start swinging the bats the way they did in separate

locales last year, and the Mets would make a legitimate run at all the other wild-card

pretenders. The boos and empty seats at Shea last night should have been enough to

tell them something else.

Chapter 4

MIKE GETS GRAND STAND

August 23, 1998

"I think that whole situation is getting a little redundant. You've got to keep things in perspective and do the best you can. That's all I did. Early on maybe I was putting a little too much pressure on myself to try and do too much. Now I'm kind of settled in."

—*Mike Piazza*

BY RALPH VACCHIANO

While New York gets itself dizzy trying to decide whether to love or hate Mike Piazza, the free-agent-to-be has somehow remained above the fray. All he's done lately is what he was expected to do all along—**be the most dangerous hitter the Mets have.**

Yesterday he did it again, launching a grand slam in the second inning to help the Mets beat the Arizona Diamond-backs, 9-4. And for that he earned a standing ovation from the Beanie Baby-enhanced crowd of 42,654 at Shea—one inning after they booed him for striking out with runners on first and third.

But such is the bizarre fate of Piazza. One minute the schizophrenic Mets fans want to give him the keys to the city. The next minute they want to change the locks.

"I think that whole situation is getting a little redundant," Piazza said. "You've

got to **keep things in perspective and do the job the best**

you can. That's all I did. Early on maybe I was putting a little too much pressure on myself to try and do too much. Now I'm kind of settled in."

Since arriving in New York in late May, Piazza has gotten a hit in 62 of 78 games and, after yesterday's 2-for-4 performance, is batting .324 (93-for-287) as a Met. His grand slam, which landed just in front of the picnic area in left, was Piazza's 23rd homer of the season and 14th as a Met. It was also his major-league-leading fourth grand slam of the season (with three as a Dodger). The rest of the Mets have none.

Piazza even played a little defense, catching Bernard Gilkey stealing in the first inning and following his slam with a sliding catch on a foul pop that sent him falling into the Arizona dugout in the top of the third. So really, what's not to like?

"That was one heck of an effort for a guy who has played a lot and is as tired as anybody out there," Manager Bobby Valentine said. "He did a great job."

For the Mets, the win continues a hot streak, which is now more than a month old. They're 24-11 in their last 35 games, and thanks to Houston's win in Chicago yesterday, they hold a one-game lead over the Cubs in the wild-card race.

But the Mets aren't just in a wild-card race right now; they also seem to be in the middle of a referendum on whether Piazza should stay at the end of the season or go.

"In New York City we have Broadway, we have Carnegie Hall, and we have some of the finest sports arenas in the world," Valentine said. "There's not one performer in any one of those arenas who goes out and wants, enjoys, tolerates, or can handle the fans' disapproval. No one wants that."

"It is interesting how a guy can be hitting three-something with 20-something home runs and get booed," John Olerud said. "But I just think they look at him as a superstar player, and he shouldn't make an out [with runners on base]."

Lately, Piazza has been coming through in those situations. And that's why yesterday

he was treated like New York's favorite son.

Chapter 5

METS' OWN MVP

September 6, 1998

"**Maybe now all the Met fans who became instant Piazza experts when he got to town on May 23 finally understand what they are seeing, what everybody always saw in Los Angeles. Maybe now people have figured out that five slow weeks in New York did not wipe out five star seasons in L.A.**"

—*Mike Lupica*

BY MIKE LUPICA

He got three hits on Friday night, his birthday, and hit a home run into the night to beat the Braves. Yesterday Mike Piazza got another big hit, broke up a double play and got the Mets a big run. He is at .344 as a Met, with 20 home runs and three more weeks to play.

Finally, he carries the team. The past few weeks he has carried his team the way Sammy Sosa carries his. Sosa fights with Mark McGwire for baseball history, with Piazza for the wild card in the National League.

Maybe now all the Met fans who became instant Piazza experts when he got to town on May 23 finally understand what they are seeing, what everybody always saw in Los Angeles. Maybe now people have figured out that five slow weeks in New York did not wipe out five star seasons in L.A.

Remember something: No one outside New York knew the Mets were still in

the league before Piazza got here. After the Mets won Friday night, I called the

Elias Sports Bureau and got these numbers: The Mets were averaging 18,177 fans

before May 23. Since then, they are averaging more than 35,000. You do the math.

Of course there are more reasons than just Piazza. School gets out, the weather

gets better, the Yankees play three games, McGwire comes to town, the team ends

up in a real good wild-card race. **But the real Mets season started**

with him, from that sellout his first day. Even when he wasn't

driving every single runner home, people were paying attention to the Mets again.

Stars do that. People who still don't get it with him are hereby sentenced to a life-

time of watching *BASEketball*.

Before yesterday, McGwire and Sosa each had 12 home runs in his last 22 games. Piazza, with half as many home runs for the season, had eight in his last 10, and nearly a .600 batting average. Piazza tries to take the Mets to the playoffs for the first time since 1988. Sosa tries to take the Cubs for the first time since '89.

Piazza sure can't stop now. He is in there against a champ, the MVP of the National League and maybe all baseball. Sosa is not the cover boy McGwire is these days. He is a Dominican, not a Californian. All along, even as people have made passes at giving him equal time, he has been treated like somebody always coming from the outside. He keeps coming, will probably chase McGwire all the way to October, the Cubs on his back the whole time. While Piazza and the Mets chase him.

The closer McGwire gets to Roger Maris, the more he becomes

a combination of Huck Finn and Popeye the sailor. But Sosa is the

one with the more interesting back story, even if he wasn't born here.

That one is the story about a skinny 16-year-old getting off a bus

from Santo Domingo and showing Omar Minaya, now the Mets'

assistant general manager and then a Rangers scout, enough to get a

$3,500 bonus to sign. The kid had held out for $4,000.

Now he is rich, one of the most famous athletes anywhere. He

hits a home run Friday night, and it goes up on the scoreboard in

St. Louis: McGwire 59, Sosa 57. They are interested in the home runs

at Shea Stadium, but more interested that Sosa has helped the Cubs

win another game. Then Piazza hits one. The Mets win.

Piazza isn't anywhere near the Maris race. He

just gets this wild-card race.

He gets this smaller season within the long-ball

season that has belonged

to Sosa and McGwire.

FROM STAR TO CITY, BOTH SIDES SEE LIGHT

October 27, 1998

"Mets fans deserve a championship. I want to be on that championship team."

—*Mike Piazza*

The Mets made the only move they could yesterday, locking up a huge star in a star town, making the best free-agent signing for a New York baseball team since the Yankees got Reggie. But Mike Piazza, who is worth every penny of the $91 million, made an even better move. A great player like this deserves this kind of great stage, and the spotlight that comes with it. Sometimes the player needs the stage.

There are only eight players in the history of baseball who reached 200 home runs by the end of their sixth season. Of the eight, only two had a batting average of better than .300 at that time: Frank Robinson, at .302, and Piazza, whose lifetime batting average is .333. Joe DiMaggio was .347 after his first six seasons with the Yankees, 198 home runs.

The Mets kept the player they had to keep yesterday. Piazza got the place he called the

capital of the world. Everybody made the right move yesterday at Shea.

"And there are more moves to come!"

You heard that yesterday from both Mets owners, Fred Wilpon and Nelson Doubleday. And there are more moves to come, starting with Al Leiter. The Mets need more relief pitching, they need more runners on base for Piazza and more pop behind him.

But Piazza is the one. You looked out at the field at Shea, even with all the dirt behind home plate and resodding going on over by the Mets dugout, and you could already see April.

"Mets fans deserve a championship," Piazza said when it was his turn to talk on the Diamond Club level at Shea. "I want to be on that championship team."

He wanted the Mets, as it turned out, and he wanted New York, even the way

he was treated at Shea his first month in town. All the experts at reading body

language—or tea leaves—had him leaving town forever after the last game of the

Mets-Braves series. He was going to the Angels, he was going to the Orioles. He

could DH two days a week in the American League, so he was definitely going to

the American League.

And it turned out Piazza wasn't going anywhere.

Maybe it was only the money. But he sure didn't sound that way yesterday. At

a time in sports when New York City hardly ever recruits a superstar like this in the

middle of his prime, he chose New York without ever even filing for free agency.

"I knew New York was where I was meant to be,"

he said.

"I didn't want to go [anywhere else]," he said.

He said that when he went back to Los Angeles after the season, he felt himself

missing New York.

"I went back [to L.A.] and found a page had turned in my life," he said.

He came here in May and got booed and handled

that great, and now he sounded like one of our own.

He had been through something now, and came

through it like a champ. He didn't whine, even as

people who don't know him at all psychoanalyzed him

every other day. He couldn't take New York; he heard

that. He wasn't worth the money; he heard that.

Mike Piazza, who is tough, hit his way

through it all.

Best hitter in town. Best the Mets have ever

had. One of the best you will ever see. Even at Shea in

a Yankee Stadium summer, he heard enough from

New York, saw enough, to want to go the distance

here. Last May Piazza was drafted. Now

he enlists.

"It's not gonna get any easier, I

know that," he said yesterday.

Piazza has his six full seasons in the big leagues, a handful of games at the end of the '92 season. Over that time he has 200 homers, 637 RBIs, and that amazing batting average. Don Mattingly had a stretch like this once, 1984 through '89. Mattingly had a .327 average for those years, 160 home runs, 684 RBIs. In New York, no one else since Mantle and Mays in the '50s is really close.

Junior Griffey isn't available at the end of the '90s, neither is Sammy Sosa. Mark McGwire just turned 35. Piazza is 30. A catcher with numbers like these, he would have been worth

keeping at $100 million. In basketball, they give out $100 million spec contracts to kids.

The Mets started drawing again when Piazza came here. They made their run at the playoffs when he hit. They will win more next season, draw more. Bobby Valentine said once, "He is the kind of player who makes the fans feel better about the 25th player on the team."

ANTICIPATION

Yesterday he was the kind of player who made it feel like five days to Opening Day instead of five months.

You could walk right through Gate C at Shea yesterday and onto the field. You could see a Ford tractor parked in the on-deck circle. You could see Pete Flynn, the head groundskeeper, moving his guys around, checking every inch of the sod. Mostly the place was empty,

quiet, except for Flynn's voice, an occasional burst of

laughter from the guys on his crew. But in the late

afternoon, you really could see April. You could imag-

ine the place full. You could imagine it loud. You could

imagine it the way it used to be.

"Ain't this a wonderful beginning?"

Pete Flynn said, on the day

when he was supposed to be

getting Shea ready for

winter.

PIAZZA TAKES TIME TO KID AROUND

November 21, 1998

"I think it is important to become a fixture in the community, to reach out to people in general. I recognize that responsibility. I want to support the people who support the team."

—Mike Piazza

BY KENNY LUCAS

Mike Piazza hit another home run yesterday when he visited a group of sick youngsters at Schneider's Children's Hospital in New Hyde Park, L.I.

Smiles bloomed on young faces when Piazza entered a room, and only intensified when he signed an autograph or posed for a picture. Jenny Magistro, 14, of Albany, quietly clutched the pennant that Piazza had signed for her and admitted that previously she had only "sort of" been a fan of the All-Star catcher. Then, after Piazza had spoken quietly with her for a couple of minutes, things were different. "I am one now," she said.

For 90 minutes Piazza visited with the children, joking, laughing and telling them to get well. Afterward he spoke about the off-season moves made by the Mets' front office, moves that Piazza said could serve to get the Mets well—well into the postseason.

"The efforts made with Al Leiter and Dennis Cook, they're real positive," said

Piazza. **"We have a great core of guys,** and I am enthusiastic about

what we could do. With another piece or two, we can become a real World Series

team."

And if the Mets can sign additional hitters, Piazza said, the more the merrier.

"You can never have enough bats," he said. "I think we can score some runs and be exciting."

Seemingly lost in all this activity is the man Piazza replaced, Todd Hundley. Recent reports have the Mets ready to send Hundley to Baltimore for Armando Benitez. Piazza said matter-of-factly that trades are part of the business, and one day he could find himself in a similar situation.

"**Eventually, someday, someone will take my job,**" Piazza said. "I only hope I handle it with as much class as Todd. We are still very good friends, and he realized the situation. He told me, 'Don't let anyone tell you that you did it. Don't worry about me.'"

Right now Piazza need not worry about anyone taking his job. Secure with his seven-year, $91 million contract, Piazza said he is enjoying life on the East Coast.

"The support for the team is unprecedented. It's blue-collar support," he said. "The people live and die with the team. That doesn't make it better or worse [than in Los Angeles], but it is different, and I am fortunate to have been in both situations."

Piazza said it was important to him to recognize that fan support with his actions on and off the field.

"I think it is important to become a fixture in the community, to reach out to people in general. I recognize that responsibility," said Piazza. "I want to support the people who support the team."

Chapter 8

HAIL PIAZZA AS BIG CHEESE

February 21, 1999

"There's no doubt that Mike brings a different aura to our group. He's special. He's that marquee player. He's that superstar, real personable, talented and good-looking."

—*Bobby Valentine*

BY RAFAEL HERMOSO

The Mets' 1999 season began yesterday at 9:04 a.m.

Wearing shades and his trademark goatee, Mike Piazza strode into the Mets clubhouse. His clubhouse. His new home.

Wearing a white V-neck sweatshirt, blue jeans and white sneakers, Piazza was trailed by a small mob of cameramen as he walked past the manager's office.

Almost instantly, Bobby Valentine bolted from his room and made a beeline to his star catcher. And then, in a belated Valentine's Day gift, the manager planted a big kiss on the left side of Piazza's neck.

"I hope you guys didn't get that," Valentine told photographers.

His teammates treated Piazza like a king. He dropped his bags at his locker

and made the rounds, pressing flesh with the Mets family.

First came John Franco, the Mets' unofficial captain for the past nine seasons.

Then came Hideo Nomo, Piazza's former batterymate with the Dodgers.

"I don't know about my team, but it feels like very comfortable surroundings seeing the guys," Piazza said.

Valentine might be Piazza's biggest fan, after Tommy Lasorda, the former Dodger manager and Piazza's unofficial godfather. And Valentine was Piazza's strongest ally last season when Piazza was the object of derision from Mets fans. That was long before boos turned into cheers.

"There's no doubt that Mike brings a different aura to our group," Valentine said. "He's special. He's that marquee player. He's that superstar, real personable, talented and good-looking."

After yesterday's workouts, Piazza sped off the field on a chauffeured golf cart, stopping briefly in the bullpen to sign autographs.

The ride is much shorter than a year ago, when Piazza had to exit farther north to get to Dodgertown in Vero Beach. This is a quick trip from his Boynton Beach home.

Piazza's winter was spent flying from his old pad in L.A., which is for sale ("You know anybody that wants to buy it? Kevin Brown, it might be his guest home."), back to New York, where he was house-hunting, down to Florida.

But it was apparent the city had become his home.

It was there he found an inner "peace" walking through the rain and cold from his East Side apartment to the gym or dinner. Or strolling the streets of SoHo, when garbage trucks would stop and the workers would say hello. Now he's looking for a house in New Jersey.

And Piazza gave his version of his winter visit to the downtown club Veruka, where he was reportedly not allowed to enter because it was Yankee territory.

Turns out, Piazza said, he was barred initially because he was wearing sneakers. But when the bouncer saw who it was, he said, "If I let David Wells in almost naked, I can let you in."

Before Piazza signed his seven-year, $91 million contract last October, Mets co-owner Fred Wilpon told him he could become "a hero in New York forever."

Piazza claims he might not have signed with the Mets if not for last season's bizarre two-week stretch in which he was traded from the Dodgers to the Marlins to New York. It forced him to face the "unknown."

Piazza voiced no complaints when his contract was quickly surpassed, though he still seems sensitive to perceptions that he was greedy.

"I knew it wasn't going to last," Piazza said. "Two years from now, when Ken Griffey Jr. is making $20 million, people will say, 'Wow, look at that.' . . . I don't want to say I'm a bargain right now, but there's guys making a lot more money than me."

Chapter 9

PIAZZA PUTS BIG HURT ON BOARD

May 10, 1999

"That's why they pay him 90 million."

—*Bobby Bonilla, marveling at one of Piazza's home runs*

BY RAFAEL HERMOSO

After twice hitting the center-field scoreboard before the game with blasts that would have easily traveled more than 500 feet, Mike Piazza went 3-for-4 with a homer in yesterday's game. Now he gets three games at Coors Field, where he has hit .449 with 12 homers in 107 lifetime at-bats.

"The problem is I've been too anxious, swinging at some bad pitches," said Piazza, who wouldn't declare his swing completely back from the two-week layoff caused by a sprained right knee. He waved at a breaking ball the pitch before the homer.

Piazza's first batting-practice shot, off bullpen coach Randy Niemann, dented the digital scoreboard 407 feet away from home plate and about 100 feet above the field. The scoreboard, which still worked, soon read, **"Mike, Please Don't Hurt Me."**

Piazza's second titanic blast deflected off a rotating Wheel of Fortune advertisement above center field.

"That was crispy," Robin Ventura said, using one of Piazza's adjectives.

"That's why they pay him 90 million," Bobby Bonilla said.

Perhaps the best line came from

light-hitting Rey Ordonez, who said, "If

I hit it from shortstop, no chance."

Mark McGwire last year hit the

scoreboard and caused $2,000 worth of

damage and had another blast that

bounced through an open panel above

left field and onto the street.

Chapter 10

PIAZZA HAS A BLAST IN CLUTCH

July 11, 1999

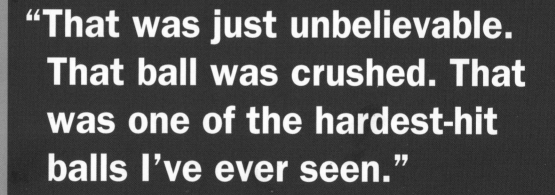

"That was just unbelievable. That ball was crushed. That was one of the hardest-hit balls I've ever seen."

—*Tino Martinez, on Piazza's 482-foot homer against the Yankees*

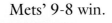

BY RAFAEL HERMOSO

Mike Piazza's short career with the Mets has seemingly been as much about long home runs as questions about his hitting in the clutch. So it's fitting that after beginning the Subway Series fielding questions about whether he was pressing, Piazza again answered back with his bat.

His 482-foot home run yesterday was outnumbered by six Yankee blasts, but it left both clubhouses in awe after the Mets' 9-8 win.

"That was just unbelievable," Tino Martinez said. "That ball was crushed. That was one of the hardest-hit balls I've ever seen. Yesterday was line-drive hard. This one was just incredible hard."

"It's the hardest-hit ball I've ever seen," said Jorge Posada, who homered

twice. "The way it carried and traveled, I didn't think it was coming down."

For the second straight day, Piazza came out for a

curtain call. Friday night, his line-drive

three-run shot into the left-field bleachers

off Roger Clemens in the sixth

inning broke a 2-2 tie

and led the Mets to their second

straight win over the Yankees.

Yesterday, his 19th homer strained

necks as the Mets clinched

their first series win

over the Yankees since interleague

play began in 1997.

After Paul O'Neill's second homer of the game had given

the Yankees a 5-4 lead in the top of the sixth, Piazza stepped to

the plate with runners on first and second and two out in the

bottom of the inning. He took a sinker for a strike, then

watched two more pitches before sending Ramiro Mendoza's

next offering toward the Whitestone for the third of five lead

changes in the game.

The towering drive finally landed on top of the picnic tent

beyond the visitors' bullpen in left field and would have left the

stadium if not for that.

"It's one of those few homers I don't

really think you can

hit any harder," Piazza

said. "It's nice to do that once

in a while. I just hope it's not

too long before I hit balls like

that."

Bobby Valentine, who likened Piazza's slump to walking through a rain forest without an umbrella, called yesterday's homer a "tent job."

That made Joe Torre's decision to intentionally walk Piazza to load the bases with two outs in the ninth a no-brainer. Matt Franco's pinch single won the game.

An exhausted Piazza, who had to watch Yankee hitters batter his pitchers all day, said after the game, "I need a nap."

The way Piazza has performed lately, it's understandable. Entering the Yankees series, Piazza, who has homered in three straight games, was hitting .222 with runners in scoring position. But in the two games against the Yankees, he is 3-for-4 in those situations, including yesterday's first-inning double with two strikes and two outs to score Rickey Henderson. "You can't go out there thinking, 'I've got to make a statement,'" said Piazza, who called himself a streaky hitter.

"You just go out and do the things you know are the right things mechanically to hit.

"I saw things weren't working, so I took a different approach," Piazza said. "I hit the home run against the Rocket [Roger Clemens] last night, and ever since that I've been swinging the bat pretty well."

Chapter 11

PIAZZA FANS GO WYLDE

October 3, 1999

While most of the fans booed Wylde's hard-core rendition of the national anthem, they wholeheartedly cheered Piazza's smash later in the game. Piazza said he dedicated the homer to Wylde.

"It was cool for me because I am an aspiring musician."

—Mike Piazza

efore one of the Mets' biggest games of the season last night, Mike Piazza got a special gift from one of his favorite musicians.

Piazza received a guitar and a few lessons from hard-rock musician Zakk Wylde of the Black Label Society. Piazza returned the favor in the eighth inning, when the slugger blasted a two-run homer to help the Mets rout the Pirates, 7-0, at Shea.

"I signed this stuff and said, 'These bats aren't worth much now, but 10 years from now they'll be worth a lot less,'" said Piazza, who gave Wylde a few bats and jerseys. "I got the better end of the deal."

Mets fans might have gotten the better end of the deal. While most of the fans booed Wylde's hard-core rendition of

the national anthem, they wholeheartedly cheered Piazza's smash later in the game.

Piazza said **he dedicated the homer to Wylde.**

"Not the first four at-bats but the last one," said Piazza, who went 1-for-5. "It

was cool for me because I am an aspiring musician."

Piazza knows he's better off sticking to his day job. Piazza's slam gave him 40 home runs and 124 RBIs for the season, tying career highs set back in 1997.

Besides his power at the plate, Piazza helped starter Rick Reed chalk up a career-high 12 strikeouts in shutting out the Pirates in such a meaningful game.

"Third or fourth inning, Mike said, 'You could have done this

all year if you just hit your spots like this,'" Reed said.

"He did everything he had to do, working both sides of the

plate and getting Rick's breaking ball into the scenario," Bobby

Valentine said. "Mike was able to keep working that in, and it made

his fastball so much better. **Just a spectacular effort**."

Besides his blast, Piazza scored one of the Mets' two runs in the sixth inning. Piazza reached first when his broken-bat hit to third resulted in a wild throw by Aramis Ramirez in an attempt to force John Olerud at second base. Piazza moved to third on a Robin Ventura RBI double and scored when first baseman Kevin Young caught a Rey Ordonez liner, only to make a wild throw to third in an attempt to double up Piazza.

In the eighth, Piazza's 368-foot homer to right brought Olerud in to give the Mets a 7-0 lead. The Mets scored five runs in that inning.

Afterward, Piazza proudly showed off his new guitar. If the Mets make the postseason, Piazza has a suggestion.

"[Wylde] should play before the playoffs," Piazza said. "A lot of people were shocked and perplexed [by the anthem]. If you listen closely, **he did an outstanding improvisation.**"

Mets fans can argue Piazza did the same last night.

Chapter 12
PIAZZA'S DAZED & CONFUSED

October 16, 1999

"There are very few opportunities you get in your career to play in a league championship series. I'm not going to let that pass by. They're going to have to carry me off the field."

—Mike Piazza

BY THOMAS HILL

Mike Piazza was hoping that last night's game against the Braves might become the special postseason moment that has been missing from his career. Instead he ended up with a costly error, a mild concussion and a very sore left hand.

The Mets moved to the brink of elimination last night at Shea, and Piazza staggered there with them. With the end possible for the Mets tonight in Game 4 of the NLCS, the best Piazza could do was express hope that he would be able to help them.

"If I feel good, I'm going to play,"

Piazza said.

Piazza, though, was unable to offer any assurance about how his head or his hand would feel this morning. He

acknowledged that he would "probably not" play in his current condition if this were the regular season.

Piazza sustained the concussion in a first-inning home-plate collision with Bret Boone. He then took a blow on the next-to-last knuckle of his left hand on a backswing by Gerald Williams in the eighth. Last night's full-contact contest came just one week after an adverse reaction to a cortisone shot caused his left hand to swell to twice its normal size.

Piazza's discomfort began in the

first, when he stepped awkwardly on home plate with his left foot while attempting

to catch Boone stealing second. Piazza slipped, his throw sailed into center field and

Williams scored the only run of the night.

Brian Jordan hit a fly ball to center. Melvin Mora made a strong one-bounce

throw home and **Piazza held onto the ball as Boone barreled**

into him. The impact sent Piazza sprawling, causing the concussion—his second

this season and at least his third in the past two years. Piazza felt woozy and nauseated when he returned to the Mets dugout but declined a suggestion by Mets trainer Fred Hina to take a rest.

"Fred said, 'If you're woozy, maybe you should come out of the game,'" Piazza said. "I said, **'No I want to play.'** There are very few opportunities you get in your career to play in a league championship series. I'm not going to let that pass by. They're going to have to carry me off the field."

It nearly came to that in the eighth, when Williams took a big swing at an 0-and-1 pitch from Armando Benitez and whacked Piazza on his left hand. In the bottom of the inning, Hina tried to manipulate the knuckle, and Piazza winced in obvious pain. X rays showed no fracture.

Piazza's encounters with Williams' bat have become an unfortunate coincidence. Williams caused one of Piazza's previous concussions when he hit him in the head with a backswing last season.

"I thought he kind of put that recoil behind him," Piazza said. "Maybe he let it go a little bit. Armando was throwing hard."

Piazza took his final at-bat against Mike Remlinger. After singling twice in his first three at-bats, he drove a fly ball to the track in right but wanted something more.

"I felt a little bit of discomfort," Piazza said. "But adrenaline has a way of helping you out in that situation. . . . **I wanted to at least take a shot at tying the game."**

Chapter 13

MIKE'S BODY
A SORE SUBJECT

October 19, 1999

"I can't explain why I am getting so banged up. It's been such a bad week. Maybe I'm doing something wrong. Maybe I should go do a good deed, help an old lady cross the street or something. Maybe something is getting back to me." —*Mike Piazza*

BY OHM YOUNGMISUK

Foul balls have hit him in the most unpleasant of areas.
Backswings have taken hard chops at his wrist. And
base runners have come flying at him at home plate like batteries at John Rocker.

Mike Piazza has absorbed so many hits to his body in this
postseason, he feels like he just boxed 12 rounds with Mike
Tyson while being bowled over by Jerome Bettis.

He's certainly got a black-and-blue left forearm to
prove it.

"It's just weird," the Mets catcher said yesterday. "I can't
explain why I am getting so banged up. **It's been such
a bad week.** Maybe I'm doing something wrong. Maybe
I should go do a good deed, help an old lady cross the street or
something. Maybe something is getting back to me."

So far in this NLCS against Atlanta, Piazza has endured two home-plate collisions—with Bret Boone and Keith Lockhart, respectively. The Boone incident resulted in a concussion for Piazza in Game 3, while the smaller Lockhart planted his batting helmet into Piazza's left forearm Sunday in Game 5, causing a muscle strain. Both times, though, Piazza hung onto the ball and made the play.

Sunday, the 6-3, 215-pound Piazza also took a blow to his left arm from a Ryan Klesko backswing, and a foul tip to the groin area.

Don't forget that he had already missed two games against Arizona in the NL division series with an inflamed left thumb.

Piazza was so battered by the 13th inning Sunday that he could play no more, giving way to Todd Pratt in the 14th. Piazza underwent X rays yesterday on his forearm. The results, however, were negative. **Just a lot of bruises and aches.**

"Mike has a pretty good black-and-blue on his arm, discoloration," Bobby Valentine said of his backstop, who is expected to play today. "But he says it feels a lot better. With the rest and [today's] game, he should be okay."

Piazza played in 140 games during the regular season, getting virtually no rest down the stretch as the Mets struggled to make the postseason.

The fatigue and injuries suffered in the postseason have severely affected his powerful bat.

Piazza, who said he won't consider playing another position in the future unless asked to, has batted just .150 (3-for-20) with one RBI, one walk and five strikeouts against Atlanta this series. He went 1-for-6 Sunday.

"If you have any pain in the fingers or thumbs or wrists or hands, it's tough because you are swinging the bat," said Piazza, whose limp left arm looked almost as if it were being held up by a sling yesterday. "Every time I move my hand, I get a lot of tingling in my fingers. Todd [Pratt, his backup] has so much energy and so much resolve that he is doing a good job. It's not like the team says, 'Oh, Mike is out of the lineup. The team doesn't have a chance.' Everybody is pulling their weight."

Piazza knows he has done his part defensively. **He just hopes he can do the same with his bat before it's all over.**

Could Piazza use a whole new left arm?

"I'm looking for a donor," he said. "Maybe I should call up Arnold Schwarzenegger."

MIKE'S ATTITUDE AND BODY HEALTHY

February 17, 2000

"After a couple of weeks or so Mike was OK and we started talking. But I never talked about the game. I'm not sure he's watched it. I watch it but not with him. I don't know if Mike could do that yet. I'm still in disbelief about what occurred. We were so close. It was so sad to see it lost that way . . . a grand slam, a base hit, anything other than to walk in the winning run. I know Mike felt destroyed."

—*Vince Piazza, Mike's father*

BY LISA OLSON

The last time Mike Piazza wore a Mets uniform, he resembled a lost little boy. All that money, all that fame, and none of it mattered. His body was a wreck, broken in a few places, bleeding in others and aching everywhere else. His voice was cracking. He had tears in his eyes. He stood in a corner of the visitors' clubhouse at Turner Field in Atlanta, stood there for a long time, refusing to sit, to take a shower, to shed his second skin. Every now and then he'd fiddle with a bat, like Linus reaching for his security blanket.

It was 2 a.m., hours after Piazza had sent a John Smoltz fastball into the stands to tie Game 6 of the NLCS at 7-all in the seventh. Piazza did not remember many of the details of that pitch, probably because the only replay from that game that mattered was the one in which Kenny Rogers walked in

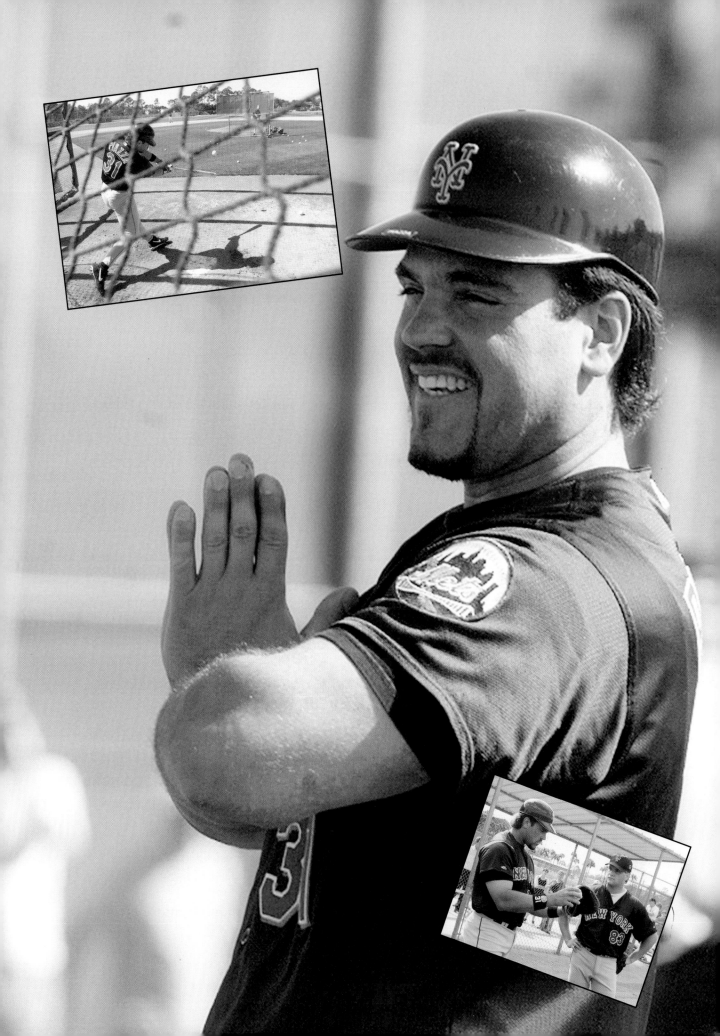

the winning run four innings later. Piazza was like a crash victim, stunned and dazed. He could only stare at the wall, glassy-eyed, and mumble mostly incoherent murmurs.

How long did that emotional hangover last? "It took a few weeks," Piazza says now. "It was tough." This is a rare glimpse into Piazza's psyche, but he quickly catches himself before revealing too much and says, "But I wouldn't trade anything insofar as the way everything occurred last year. Well, I should take that back. The thing I'd trade in is a win in Game 6."

Instead of playing Game 7—a game the Mets are convinced they would have won, because surely the baseball gods had been bowled over like everyone else—

Piazza slipped into a cocoon. **His limbs needed time to heal; so did his heart.**

"It was very devastating to him," Vince Piazza says of his son. "He just went off on his own and decided to get away from it. He didn't want to talk to anyone other than his mother."

Even 31-year-olds with $91 million contracts and the world at their feet need their moms, right? Vince nods and laughs. It is the Mets' first day of spring training, and on the other side of the fence, Mike Piazza is making the balls look as if they have wings. Vince has to raise his voice over the incessant whacks.

"After a couple of weeks or so, Mike was OK and we started talking," he continues. "But I never talked about the game. I'm not sure he's watched it. I watch it, but not with him. I don't know if Mike could do that yet. I'm still in disbelief about what occurred. We were so close. It was so sad to see it lost that way . . . a grand slam, a base hit, anything other than to walk in the winning run. I know Mike felt destroyed."

These days he looks anything but. **Full of perky smiles and contagious optimism**, Piazza arrived in camp yesterday morning still high from his trip to Vegas and the ESPY Awards, where he was touched by the tribute to the slain Columbine High teacher. The cameras love Piazza the way they love, say, Brad

Pitt. He keeps his life wrapped tightly, and still the media flock to him as if he holds the key to the secret box.

"Hey, Mike's here," shouts one of his teammates, meaning the season may officially begin. "Happy Gilmore's here."

Ah, to be like Mike. Two seasons ago, when he was playing out the final year of his contract, he took out a $15 million insurance policy on his body. If Jennifer Lopez can insure her bodacious behind for, what, a billion dollars, then it certainly behooves a baseball player to protect himself against disability. Now he is rested and buff and fully prepared to crouch behind the plate for 130-140 games this season. He never vied for the leadership position but accepts it as part of the territory. We fire off questions, searching for the World According to Mike.

"I know I'm a big part of this ball club, but by no means am I going to make the destiny of this team," he says.

Is this team better, despite undergoing a 25 percent roster change? "Oh, no question I think we're better on paper, but that's no guarantee of success on the field. We look better. We got a great pitcher [Mike Hampton], among other guys."

What does he think of the Ken Griffey Jr. trade? "I was a little confused, actually. It's obvious [Cincinnati's] a better ball club, but they're one of many teams we're going to have to worry about. Ken Griffey Jr. is a tremendous ballplayer, but as many teams have proven in the past, one player cannot make the fate of a ball club."

How about the Braves' John Rocker? Will he ever be able to play at Shea? "I mean, I don't know," Piazza says with a nervous laugh. "It's going to be tough. It's going to be difficult to weed out all the distractions. As we've shown before, it's a tremendous rivalry between two ball clubs."

Diplomatic and loquacious, Piazza is nothing like that shattered shell of a man who wore No. 31 last October. "One of the positives of this team is we were able to inspire people and cause a lot of frustrations as well," he says, and not once does he look like he needs talking in from the ledge.

An off-season in New York can soothe even the most wounded of souls. Piazza chose to recuperate in the heart of the beast. He witnessed the fans' pain. It helped heal his own.

"I absolutely feel like I'm a New Yorker," he says. "I'm all wired in with the restaurants and stuff. It's nice to go out and hit all the spots and enjoy the diversity of the city."

Who wouldn't want to have his life? Handsome and humble and richer than Bali, Piazza's the toast of New York and the backstop of a team that is pegged to do great things.